Day of the Body

Carol Frost

Ion Books, Inc./*Raccoon*
Memphis, Tennessee

Ion Books, Inc./*Raccoon*
3387 Poplar Avenue, Suite 205
Memphis, TN 38111

A *Raccoon* Book

Library of Congress Cataloging-in-Publication Data

Frost, Carol, 1948—
    Day of the body.

    I. Title.
PS3556.R596D3   1986   811'.54   86—15306
ISBN 0-938507-01-X

Cover: *In the Forest* by Henri Rousseau
        Reproduced by courtesy of Kunsthaus Zurich

Book design by David Spicer & Diana Taylor

ACKNOWLEDGEMENTS

Acknowledgements are due to the editors of the following publications in which many of these poems first appeared:

APR: "The Undressing," "Death in Winter," "Passage," "Cold Frame," and "Late Sigh"
Antaeus: "The Salt Lesson" and "Liar's Dice"
bits: "The Cemetery is Empty"
Chariton Review: "Aubade of an Early Homo Sapiens"
Denver Quarterly: "The Gardener Envies Henri Rousseau"
Georgia Review: "Harriet St."
Iowa Review: "Girl on a Scaffold"
Ironwood: "Redbirds"
Kansas Quarterly: "The Whispering Geese"
Kenyon Review: "The Haircut"
Mademoiselle: "Unfinished Song"
Massachusetts Review: "Getting it Right"
Missouri Review: "Sovereign Bear," "To Kill a Deer," and "The Migration of Butterflies"
Montana Review: "The Winter Without Snow"
Nebraska Review: "Prayer for my Son"
New England Review: "Packing Mother's Things"
Northwest Review: "The New Dog: Variations on a Theme by Jules Laforgue," "The Gardener Must Mow Near the Dead Rabbit," "The Gardener Delivers a Fawn," and "The Gardener Praises Rain "
Pequod: "The Homemade Piano" and "Autumn Apology"
Poetry Northwest: "Abnormal Song"
Poetry NOW: "Klimt's Baby"
Prairie Schooner: "The Day of the Body," "The Light Asks," "Snake Skins," and "A Field Full of Black Cats"
Quarterly West: "Notes to the Cold"
Raccoon: "The Embroidery"
Seneca Review: "Deerhorns"
Shenandoah: "The Scar" and "Our Night"
Tendril: "Mallard"
West Branch: "Carousel"

Some of these poems were published in small editions from Graywolf and Ithaca House.

Two paintings by Paul Gauguin, *The Spirit of the Dead Watching* and *D'ou venons nous? Que sommes nous? Ou allons nous?* inform the title poem.

I want to thank Richard Frost, Dorothy Bloom, Bob Bensen, and Stephen Dobyns for their articulate criticism, and Jan Stankiewicz for all that typing.

CONTENTS

In Memory of Mary Nankivel

. . . thou among the wastes of time must go

I

All Summer Long

The dogs eat hoof slivers and lie under the porch.
A strand of human hair hangs strangely from a fruit tree
like a cry in the throat. The sky is clay for the child
    who is past
being tired, who wanders in waist-deep
grasses. Gnats rise in a vapor,
in a long mounting whine around her forehead and ears.
The sun is an indistinct moon. Frail sticks
of grass poke her ankles,
and a wet froth of spiders touches her legs
like wet fingers. The musk and smell
of air is as hot as the savory
terrible exhales from a tired horse.

The parents are sleeping all afternoon,
and no one explains the long uneasy afternoons.
She hears their combined breathing and swallowing
salivas, and sees their sides rising and falling
like the sides of horses in the hot pasture.

At evening a breeze dries and crumbles
the sky, and the clouds float like undershirts
and cotton dresses on a clothesline. Horses
rock to their feet and race or graze.
Parents open their shutters and call
the lonely, happy child home.
The child who hates silences talks and talks
of cicadas and the manes of horses.

The Haircut

When the boy's head is heavy with his own secret
cap of hair, his mother calls him to her,
asking him to tell her about his day.
When last she called him from the depths
of the wood and combed with slender fingers
the golden current of his hair, the white
of his hidden brow, like a headstone,
had made her almost cry.
After she cut his hair, his head was quick
as a deer turning in a field to face new danger.
By the light raining down in a field in August's waste,
by the antique vase about to be knocked over
by his child's elbow, by her own perfume
lasting in the room after they leave,
can she explain her pity for him,
his forehead full of blond mysteries?

The Salt Lesson

Looking inside the bony plate, perceive
the gray sponge matter that from its depth
breeds without moving.
Colors belong to the surface, reckon
with the wind mounting tidal waves,
clouds' cover, or a ripple of sun.

Underneath, the seeping calculation,
the dark crevasses and only spots of artificial
light. What the mind allows, sucks
without bloat. Unearthly life,
a grouper eats a man whole, the gold
doubloons; something precious,

spontaneous. The gull returns to the sea
food broken down by sharks.
The mind is a sullen scavenger
with the belly and bowels of a god.

Water city, this impure taker
returns so little, a bubble of stupidity,
a salt piece of itself, of what it endures.

The Heron

A woman and her children are on a lake.
The woman steadies a rowboat
by bracing her legs against the bulkheads
and with oars that are like extensions
of her arms, as if there were no boat
and she stood in twenty feet of water.
Each time one of her children jumps off,
she is rocked back a few feet.
The lake's shades of blue are interlarded
with cool whites and greens, but the woman's eyes
instead of reflecting the water
are as clearly blue as the open air,
as if she sees without shadows,
her gaze quiet and reaching as a formation
of birds. And when the younger child
says that she is too far away, she scolds him,
saying she will never leave him
alone out there, that all he has to do
is flutter-kick a little stronger. That evening,
on shore, his face small and white
like the ivory back of a hand mirror,
he asks her outside to see the blue heron.
They watch it descend in slow spirals
until it is lost against the dark pines,
and they must imagine its flight,
which might seem to him like a drawn-out
song of parting, each level a lower note,
the last a small white finale of water
and to her a darkening hunt
for fish and frogs. It depends on her look.
Nothing else will tell him.

She wants to stay there and not break
the silence, not look like anything
until he answers his questions,
like taking himself in his own arms,
remembering a time so solid
he could stand in the dissolving
day we know no more of than going.

Prayer for my Son

My thinking that you could lie in my hands
quietly, makes it so.
You become my whispered words, almost
a prayer in my interlocking hands.

So little of what
I see is what you are. Fingernails,
cartilage, cell deaths, layers of skin,
the garden in your head:
wild pig, the air's dragons,

a humming thick as honey just below sense,
and the picked castles of bone
which held essences once, and still do. There,
the animals look at you as if you were an angel,
which is to say they will not look.

Your sleeping head heavy on my lap,
the flower of your ear tilted
in involuntary sunlight,
I ask that it could be so

for you to waken day after day
like a traveler: lonely as you'll always be,
tired, beaten, perhaps,
but smiling with ease
and a little in awe of everything.

Carousel

A chestnut gelding and a rider balancing,
the blossom-smells, manure, late summer,
and the wooden ring they ride in—
I remember this and the weightless hands
at the horse's neck, impelling
the horse to canter, horse and rider
carving a circle in the dirt and air,
the stride and matched bearing becoming metaphor
for a carousel, gilt and red, forever
turning, as the hands are metaphor
for the still heart's wings, except
the horse's head tossed,
except they wheeled and suddenly leapt
over a cross-rail, trespassing
the dust that eventually must settle
on rump and riding hat,
leapt like pursuers after the sun
just cresting the morning
hills, leapt like my heart on some days
when I see made muscular and simple
the harmony and breaking down
of such harmony that is the passing world.

The Gardener Must Mow Near the Dead Rabbit

The disembodied birds
following their stored-up songs through the swale
remind the gardener
how easily the grasses grow
because their stems are hollow;
and the spreading stain, green and black,
of the crushed rabbit, its bones no longer
well fused, so so much light leaks from a rib,
makes the gardener think
each time the mower rounds the yard
how summer comes to arias in the undergrowth—
the absent birds—and to goldenrod,
seed gushing under the wheels and blade.
As open as the gardener's pores
and glands, the rabbit's hazel eyes—
and there is no swerving of the mower.

The New Dog: Variations on a Text
by Jules Laforgue

I.   The new dog's sugary breath warms my neck,
milkflecks on his muzzle.
Day begins, lighting his lavender eyes.
Relaxed as a child, he seems to look
out across the yard at the sun's ascent.

The hour of last dreams when the bare elm
is tinged with gold. With this dog Max
I look out across the yard. I think
of newborn everywhere.
I think of Max who will wander
with curiously human eyes in the roses;
then imagine myself coming out of the garden,
going in place of Max to the road
and walking under a car.

I imagine entering this grave:
the full weight of Max counterposed against
the glance he turned away.

II.   You shovel the graveyard dirt too far
as if it were obscene to dig
a hole for Max, who is lying there
beside the rose bower, his ribs
and heart unstirred, his eyes
wide-open, tinged by the sunrise.

The hour of reverie when the elm
is lit with gold. The day begins.
Think of Max in another realm
too remote for touch, wandering in
a garden. Think of his dark eyeball
surveying darkness for us all.

Now the grave must be
refilled with the full weight of Max.
Beyond the sky's blue filigree
you cannot see the zodiac
when with sunlight in the air
you cover up his final stare.

Web-making

A spider sways along that wondrous slur,
its own silk, thrown from columbine to undiscovered
columbine, and when the cat's moony head
destroys the suspension, the spider
levitates to another flower to loop, in the quiet,
something like a line drawing of a constellation,
botanical, feeling with its 8 legs
for the tensile strength, as the mind plays with theorems.

Sometimes the spider, small as a fingertip, as a star
    beyond one's finger,
on its silk swing swings up high
and winks away.

To study the spider and its web-making
you need a random sample of many
and a delicate telescope to watch the garden, the
    columbine.
They habitually spin at night.
Dawns you can feel their wet, invisible lines
cross your skin. That's when you notice
the apparent chasms they must cross, and think the
    natural world
and the quantum heavens of crab, ram & bear
are as the Ancients saw them in the mind's eye,
pulled most delicately
together by silk inventions. What is a web?

Something time takes to finish, or to break
or to become the way things look in.

A Field Full of Black Cats

Cats in fields sit
still as idols
catching sunlight
catching moles.

Through the broken lattice-
work of grasses
they stare for hours, black
pelts burning.

One can imagine
in the belly
of each cat's shadow
a mole being

held in thrall, completely
taking the sun down
to earth, making
new terrain:

skies muscadine,
grass like tongues,
stones coughed-up
balls of fur.

Death is irremediable
here. There is no
reaching into the heart
of violence

when the catpaw sweeps
suddenly toward
the mole. The onyx
and yellow eyes

take the uptwisted flower
in as nothing
when the cats walk back
to porches

to lick themselves and drowse,
the hunched-up moles
having ended
in their hot mouths.

Getting it Right

An arthritic she-goat cannot settle
to the packed earth unless hands sway
her bag of milk out of her knees' way.
This woman has never touched
a goat, the distended pouch so much like a child's belly.
But the dignified getting half-way down and
    inevitably up,
like a failure to depart,
or an image of the slack carcass hung like a wet coat
of a person in a hurry,
overcomes her finickiness about the stench
of strong milk and goats' meat.
She straddles the goat,
lifts her as the sun rolls overhead,
and tries to get it right.

Harriet St.

The fadedness of stone
markers shows the wear
of weather. And hers,
long life near a yard of bone.

She's naked and weeds
her garden, and seems to stare at nothing.
The hot wind swings
its sharpened sickle where dark deeds

jumble with good, and begun
things end. The wing a vandal
lopped off from a stone angel
props itself on her porch in the sun.

This bears deep looking into,
all the appearances of madness
and death, or is it just coincidence,
the ancient crone, not dressed, the few

artifacts of grief
strewn on Harriet Street
across from the cemetery? In this heat
perfect connections of belief

come easily. But look.
All her dresses blow
on a clothesline. She may not bow
to earth from burdens, but to pluck

what spasms of flowers
and gems there are,
most sweet, most stolen, where
near to the living, graves are.

The Embroidery

Grandmother embroiders the summer day.
She sits amid the bodies and light of childhood,
lilac-scented, perspiring,

sewing life-like flora in cloth the color of cream.
Pollen is strewn in the air.
Some spices her hair.

The design on the porch sofa isn't far off
from the green and golden scene,
a water-garden, she inextricably sews into new cloth.

To look at her face, you would not see birth or death,
but even as hands stitch the fictitious daylight,
a drop of her blood like dew forms

and falls among the mass of raised flowers.
For the second she looks perplexed; you see both.
She sucks her finger, and brushing it on her apron

continues. A pitcher of lemonade
is on the table, a parakeet clatters in its ornate cage,
and mildew casts its net around.

The Homemade Piano

The minstrel peers through tiny eyeglasses
the size of tears at Bach
and with fantastic concentration reduces
the grand scale to fit his homemade piano—
a melancholy squeezed down from his brow
to say, "Yes, I have enough," or, "No,
I haven't enough."

He wags his fingers up and down like sticks
fastened with a hinge to the knuckles,
but his music
stays in the passerby's head
like the sense of heaviness in the hand
though a pail being carried home
is half-spilled.

In the polyphony of one little keyed instrument
there are remembered perfumes, caesuras,
and the oriole whose vowels
bewilder each morning with fortunate
and unfortunate decrees.
A rustle moves through the audience.
Here on a homemade piano is the empty heart

and full heart in counterpoint.
Tomorrow the minstrel will set
his simple box on another street corner.
If his strain still haunts,
you may find him there and ask him
why his song has no ending
and why so lovely. He'll play the variations.

The Day of the Body

I.   If a model

      If a model is posed by a sunny window
      and the artist is in love with light,
      he draws the white white vitals
      of her body in sweeping unbroken curves
      as if she were made of threads,
      but if the artist is in love with flesh
      and wishes to remain chaste,
      she possesses for him all her animal beauty
      in a belly and hips that are lit
      as if by wingfuls of warm air
      a day-sparrow caught in the sheaves.

II.   She thinks of love

Wanting to suggest a wild and luxuriant soul
and her dignity, she molds her body
after Eve's. She sees herself
by a shaded brook; a dark purple road
and green foreground, where she
undresses. She looks at her belly,
then presses there with her hand open
until she can press no more,
and the ridges of fatty tissue
between her fingers are just fat enough.
Then, like Eve, she puts on
her lips an ironic smile
and lies down and thinks of love
which means of someone she has seen.

III.   The man and the woman

The man and the woman
have been getting to know each other,
and now they are going to make love.
The bed represents the unlighted parts
of a picture, and their desire
seems to act as a wandering beam of light
that weaves around their thighs.
His hand defines the turning of her hips
just as her hips make his hands
their reality. Whether like tree trunks
or earth or light-filled air,
their bodies are caught up in a feeling
they do not quite understand: Four dark
eyes surprised by each other in a room.

IV.   So when he leaves

They aren't violent, so when he leaves
in the middle of the night
he says, tomorrow morning will be
like any other morning. He leaves her
lying on a light chrome-yellow sheet
only slightly indecent, as if she's bathed
in lamplight. After falling asleep
she sees a native girl on her belly,
showing a portion of her frightened face.
The background is purple,
a color of terror, but in the dream
she cannot tell what the girl is afraid of.
Perhaps she is thinking of someone dead
or that death is thinking of her.

V.   Where are you going?

The looser his skin gets,
the more he gets used to his soul
flying in a frequently squalid room
like a bird. All the windows are closed,
and he is the child who ducks
each time the bird whirs by. With every fiber
the child wants to free the sparrow,
there is strain around his eyes;
but it will not light, and to the boy
the bird is unpredictable, may change
its circular flight and crash into his head.
Sooner or later the boy will be brave
and rush to the door and open it.
"Where are you going?" the boy will call,
and the bird may sing, but no answer.
The boy will become a white dot
in a field, and the bird a vapor.

II

Autumn Apology

Already the land is starting to forget gardens.
The dew, no longer sweet, glazes the latticed woods
with an unreal brilliance,
so the eyes must be shielded.
Reminiscences no longer hold the heart completely,
as someone held me a little roughly
once in somber deep groves.
Gold and silver lacquers
can't jail leaves in trees or warmth in the air.
The touch I was utterly dissolute to,
that caused collapse behind my knees,
sunslides in the lake,
is unconjurable.
Bits of the world, leaves, songs
scatter in painted light.
The days
break.

The Undressing

They took off their clothes 1000 nights
and felt the plaster of the moon
sift over them, and the ground roll
them in its dream. Little did they know
the light and clay and their own sweat
became a skin they couldn't wash away.
Each night bonded to the next,
and they grew stiffer. They noticed this
in sunlight—there were calluses,
round tough moons on their extremities,
shadows under their eyes,
and sometimes a sour smell
they hadn't had as children.
It worried them, but at night the animal
in their bodies overcame their reluctance
to be naked with each other,
and the mineral moon did its work.
At last when they woke up and were dead,
statues on their backs in the park,
they opened their mouths
and crawled out, pitifully soft and small,
not yet souls.

Girl on a Scaffold

Her neck in a noose, the girl stands
on a scaffold with two officers and her lover.
She looks at the pale orchard or twilight
or the limb where a bobwhite's whistle
seems to originate. Whether the others hear
this fluting ahead of the wind can't be said
by the look on the girl's face.
The officer who is tightening the thick cord
watches the girl's brown eyes blink
several times and admires her courage
as well as her eyes which are brown as burnt loaves
of bread. Her neck is long and white,
and for a moment he wishes he could release her,
lift her into his arms and forget
how this day will end, but as he dreams
of their embrace on cool sheets, he sees himself
encircling her neck with his own rough hands
and realizes he has twisted the knot
at her tender nape too tightly.
As for the lover, he is no coward but
his throat is strangled and he is afraid
he will make a noise when she dies,
so he begins to hum a patriotic song,
the song stammering him; his hands are tied.
The other officer slaps him, and that is when
the bobwhite flies up where there was a knob
at the end of an apple bough. The bird
seems to blossom in the dying light,
and the girl's craned head lolls to one side.
With eyes shut she sees the hand grenade
leave the partisan's hand, then the colonel
leaning against the baked earth wall
putting on his socks. He was smiling

as if he knew how simple life is. Within her now
a feeling rises like the soft clashing of wings
to be free of red clay and the world twisted
by intent. Barefaced, in a soiled dress,
she stands on the trap door, heels together,
and listens for the last note of the bobwhite,
as if it were her dignity she strained for.
Shadows drain from the orchard
and gather at the base of the scaffold
as if a crowd of vague angels
had come to watch her fall.

Liar's Dice

Used to mark a corner, a claim,
these totem rocks are painted into faces,
men. I have this stamp of land
with creeping jenny, jack-in-the-pulpit,
fir trees and deep grass
I would not sell in a famine.

One way of ownership
is not to tell how much you have.
Liar's dice, the number of birds' bones
and thighs of foxes that click
on the table of the field I hold.
The checkered wind.

                    The gamble to sleep
with him when someone walking
with the cool moon or in broad day
may walk into our outdoor room
and fall on us like police.

Stood like a grizzly, emblem mask
to warn away intruders, the pole reminds.
I hide and shape my place,
own each pebble, use it all.
The beautiful fish, the warm birds.
Even if shown, love, they don't know.

Deerhorns

Amid the cattail in the calm marsh
two hunters watch two deer as dusk,
ice-gray like stars' debris, falls on
their horns. Below, dogs bark, cars rush,
but those who graze seem unaware
through the medium of the moonlight
of noise that for hunters must seem alarms
to deer whose fabled sense of the slight
stirring of wind or bloodtide tacit
beneath the bronzes of the bow-
man's coat sends them to the forest.
The hunters lie two body lengths
to match the black gold deers' repose,
and dare not move or whisper:
Would the deer drift close enough
to kill, or turn invisible
like the dissolution of an autumn?—
their mortal antlers grace a wall,
or flare like wings along the still
and withered field that bears the moon
and holds them and lets them go?
The vast twinned horns raise toward
the hunters under the wheeling sky
so every accidental sign accorded
deer of immortality seems true.
Before the wind they snort, then run
through intervals of darkness, up

the ancient tracks that flicker and slant,
while the hunters stare after
as if measuring the emptiness of hands
where a wild thing once has been,
and as if to take a deer were to have
a taste of life, its opened chest;
its eyes, small double star, gone out;
its head; and from a tranquil brow
its sense of universe: the lifted horns.

To Kill a Deer

Into the changes of autumn brush
the doe walked, and the hide, head and ears
were the tinsel browns. They made her.
I could not see her. She reappeared, stuffed with apples,
and I shot her. Into the pines she ran,
and I ran after. I might have lost her,
seeing no sign of blood or scuffle,
but felt myself part of the woods,
a woman with a doe's ears, and heard her
dying, counted her last breaths like a song
of dying, and found her dying.
I shot her again because her eyes
were open, and her lungs rattled like castanets,
then poked her with the gun barrel
because her eyes were dusty and unreal.
I opened her belly and pushed the insides
like rotted fruit into a rabbit hole,
skinned her, broke her leg joints under my knee,
took the meat, smelled the half-digested smell
that was herself. Ah, I closed her eyes.
I left her refolded in some briars
with the last sun on her head
like a benediction, head tilted on its axis
of neck and barren bone; head bent
wordless over a death, though I heard
the night wind blowing through her fur,
heard riot in the emptied head.

Stags and Salmon

*Paleolithic drawing from
the grotto of Lortet, France*

A hint of fear
in the over-the-shoulder stare,
the mouth open not for chewing.
And hunters have come
to push the stags across the waters.
Of this succession,
bone and pearly space,
the artist caught
salmon like quarter moons
and placed them by the stags.
This is the drawing where
the beauty of relation begins.
A stag, carved round an antler,
turning its head, its antlers
crisp as flames,
and before it a running buck
crowded by salmon.
I think they must be swimming,
the lake water so clear
it cannot enter the design.

The Snake Skins

The intrigue of this house
is a snake in the foundation, disturbed once
out of his stone place
by a laborer who was removing part of the floor

and southern wall, its lath and crumbling plaster,
to add a sliding glass door.
There were five or six shed skins,
like a multiplication

of the snake's slithering
so close beneath the whispers the night
provoked us to hear and our bare feet.
Now, though more variance of light

pours into the century-old house, flux
and equinox,
and though the laborer cut in half the snake,
I think in darkness, deep in the recesses

of air and dust, in edifices
thought solid, of the little motions
going on, breeding snakes that may
and may

not be meek. I only know
of the spotted adder dead long ago
and these skins like gloves for individual fingers.
I suspect there are others.

Packing Mother's Things

I put into a carton the unstrung doll
wrapped in a baby quilt
whose eyes open and shut with a thunk
as the lids strike the molded brow
with the resonance of a hammer inside a clock.
I also put in an old radio,
shaped like the grille of a late-model car
whose singers sang *O Careless Love*
and *Lulu's Back in Town*.
Then I put in the inedible cake
and the tiny wax couple all in black.
Then the cameo. In the cameo a woman is etched
in shell, four folds to her skirt,
and she is holding one fold as she steps
and waves goodbye. The sky is abalone.
The two faintly Chinese buildings have a window
for looking out and a door for welcome.
But the woman, white as a cemetery in snow,
inaudible as a saved letter in a secret compartment
of a desk, is bidding goodbye.
I call the Goodwill and say
that they can have everything else.
But they won't take the windows, the doors,
the bathroom and the lawn;
they slide the mattresses down the stairs.
They are incredulous that I would leave
her shag rug red as cabbage, an aviary,
a homemade bookcase.
One of them finds a piece of scrap paper
and says, This is someone's,
don't you want it, I think it's a poem.

The Cemetery is Empty

The stones are streaked
as if a community had stood
and wept away all cause for tears.
Verses, names have rained into graves,
and the pain has come apart
like a very old doll in the finder's hands.

All I Cannot: Mirror Soliloquy

Your slender well-formed body bends
in a movement of clipped flowers falling,
to rub the dust off its shoe. I've seen you
bathing, washing, drying yourself,
your breasts cretonne and right in the basin;
felt your presence in a room long before
you arrived; stalked you with a sort of cold fever
only by standing silent where a little light was.
Now I crouch to dust my shoe, knowing this
is your gesture. As I stand, you look
in my direction, jaw frank, eyes blue and marble
like the small astronomy photos of the earth
on the coffee table. The earth moves 648,000 miles
per hour in orbit around the sun. Light flings
from source to shadow at 186,000 miles per second.
I have felt your forehead pressed to mine
and seen the delta wing of your breath dissolve,
scintillant curve. Is this how a song is left
that no longer sings? Is a tear first a ray
of your coloring inside your head? Is a mind
the fire of nothing when you close your eyes?
You frown and walk away, not clay,
not bone, not sweat, yet bound in these
as I am glassbound. You pause by the door
as if you understand me, might let me be
uncaged, the least amount of light
escaping from a mirror; but with a gesture
to behead the violets on the table,
you cut the light and leave. The ebony
fling of darkness is upon me.
Surely I was, that once happened, a shape
frilling at the crown of an infinite hollow:
our difference: all I cannot see.

Late Sigh
for A G

As desultory sunlight
slants across concertgoers and the lake,
the Italian man,

bald, in wool pants, one jowl
tumored, plays like an angel, brutally
the aeolian riffs—every swell and change

or hoarse gush of Autumn
fare-you-well.

It doesn't have to be narrative—the unloved
wife is dead, the Whiteman band all gone—
for them to hear

as in the ears of the old musician
the sad and beautiful profanities
of jazz: how everything gone turns rare.

Even now the indrawn
late sigh of the saxophone

stirs the gray-green leaves of ash
and breaks like a bubble
on the lake,

as if you and he
should feel lucky you are alive.

The Tumored Angel

His wings whir more slowly,
weary of holding him halfway between alabastrine
vacancy and a pile of hills. He thumps down hard,
humming a sarabande
he's been taught for materializing. His body's
in a sheet, no scrotum, no shoes.
Docile and radiant, he peers
into a trailer window at television
noise and the blue light, at people hiding,
it seems to him from the cold glory
of fall's sunrise. They're looking at a soap opera.

It's the same story.
The angel is supposed to touch one of them
on the shoulder, these amateur believers,
and in a moment of recognition, like knowing the yelp
    of hounds
is geese, he or she will sense God's
mastery. This angel doesn't like
easy conversions; he too was a man
fluttering toward salvation, as a moth flutters
toward bright lights and destruction.

He changes from veil to flesh
and indicates the tumored hollows of himself
with the sign of the cross. If the believer
reaches in and touches gold, the promised
Paradise, as surely as lights go out, will disappear,

but feeling tumor, he will be reminded of all
the places, drawn quivering and cold,
that cannot be called good unless
someone reaches in and touches and is moved.

The angel squirms when touched (another ploy?)
and thinks of monks in hell; he pictures his insides
as lumps of dead roe and Time burning in coal
blue day. But in his face the heart's color comes,
in his earth-brown eyes the world.
Then he passes without a word
through the diminishing sculptures of trees.
The smell of cold leaves scarcely names the event,
and the angel, knowing he is deathless, pauses
before the long climb zenithward, wanting to feel
upon his shoulders not wings, but the weight of wind.

III

Death in Winter

Dropped in straw
in a barn lagged against winter,
the lamb had vertigo.
With no malice the lamb's mother

moved away.
The lamb hobbled and bleated in dark
cold sanctuary,
knelt like a monk, then stepped crooked

toward crooked light.
It leapt through the torn boards without
fear or deliberate
reflection. In its eyes the slight

snow threshold
had blazed like some beheld heaven.
Then deepening cold
and ice grown in its eyes like stone.

Great snow fell
onto soughing trees. Softly
snow stroked the curly wool.
A balm of snow swept in mercy.

The lamb's gaze,
rolled in, envisioned all sweetness
and lasting light: the brain's
pure honeycomb had crystallized.

The Scar

Phrenologists and doctors know
beyond this symmetry of quartz-weight,
this living skull, yours, flourishes darkness.

A diabolical, queer knot of cells
has come to nest (large as a hummingbird
nest) behind your ear,

migrating from a lung.
When they took your skull apart,
it fit back perfectly, locking

like restored pyramids.
Your cobalt-treated head drops
gray flakes. You wear a wool cap

and worry the radiation's damaged hair-roots.
There is such little terror in your eyes,
though your brain outgrows itself.

Your memory outgrows itself:
all you have held and lost. Dragon
kimono and iridescent butterfly tray

from Japan you brought to a sweetheart.
Wartime memories *Esquire* nearly published.
A love affair in Detroit.

As you ask me to trace the scar,
I see a mark of wings, snow hieroglyphic,
mapping its possession as moonlight

sometimes possesses the earth.
And, darkness outgrowing itself, a vanishing.
As I touch your milky head, you smile,

your eyes blue as the sky you will soon lose.

The Light Asks

It is a cold dawning and remarkably light out,
like from bed in his childhood, windows down to the
    floor.
The trees are tight as candlesticks in a box,
candles for the special occasions.

Slinging his rifle more squarely,
he looks at the stark white toes of his boots,
then at the sky. High in an oak
the nest of a large bird moves like an animal.

He walks to the dark circumference
of the tree, taps the trunk, and looks up it.
The coon is there, hugging a high limb.
His father told him to climb, and he climbs.

He'd had something like a dream once
when his parents were sleeping,
to paint his room, his bed, and his little brother
in the crib. Afterwards, the brush

in his hand, he'd said a "cop"
told him he could paint, and he could.
He tests the branches with his hands and legs,
the dead ones the color of rake handles,

his eyes on the tree. When he looks up
for the coon, his mind slips,
and he falls like wood toward the roots.
His thigh wedges where a shaft of light had been.

His leg is foreign to him on impact;
and later when pain
comes like a stiff wind breaking through the woodlot,
he tries to disown it. Every second

he pauses, deciding, light breaks away
from the far hills,
and he thinks, What now, Mom?
He watches the sunlight freeze on his thigh.

There are no answers in woodcraft
for this, and his father is not coming
to get him. Evening rolls out its dark carpet.
He faints.

When he wakes, the light asks
who he is. The owls begin their calling in the silence.
He can't turn from the arms that hold him;
he thinks of the sweet peace of sleep.

No one is there to whisper him awake
until he is too deep in himself to be called to.
His rifle lies where it has fallen in snow.
Above him, light moves as branches.

The Stone Child

Beneath the ice he is a lost work
by Michaelangelo, stone cold
upon the river's mud
and fully clothed in Newberry's
jeans, coat, and skates.

Whether by the extremes
of youth or glacial waters,
time more fabulous than the tar-
pit's is caught and slowed
under the bright bars of the stream.

He breathes his own blood,
choking, while rubber-booted firemen
saw the ice, and the setting sun
through a line of trees
gravely builds its scaffold.

He has slain giants, and is slain.
His dark eyes are blank.

I saw them haul
a youngster out of his drowned pool
once, his face blue as marble.
One beat his chest, another
breathed into him with all

the jagged tenderness
that endears air and stone.
I thought if he should begin
again to live,
freed from the hardened surface

of another element,
like a tiger from snow,
a trilobite walking in amber, a window
would open into the dark-eyed abyss,
dividing it into places and moments.

The sprigs of his hair
were frozen. He held on helpless
as if from the beginning his breath
had been borrowed
and would soon belong to another.

In the beginning, in the beginning—
his lungs bubbled
and expelled
the gray water. How much was
what he thought, how much nothing

if he no longer did?
He was beautiful as the next boy,
beautiful as David, looking as if he
could with a simple gesture
be made to move. And he lived,

suffering to be stonelike,
scraped of all but being there,
a fossil of departure.
      He has slain giants, and is slain.
      His dark eyes are blank.

Too much time has passed.
They ought to let him be
part of the ending he
was always skating heedlessly toward.
To remain, a step behind, is the harder task.

The Whispering Geese

Because we know it's only a matter of time
before the whispering geese reach the end of the river,
their webs inextricable from the vast
platform of blazing ice, wings raised
in a suggestion of escape,
we imagine the sounds they make make sense,
could we listen in the right way.
If we stopped and thought *death* with no hope
to gather into one whole or fragmented message
the secret sense of several hundred
geese plummeting to the hard rock
bottom of the falls, each in its own spotlight
of ice, the crashing tonnage
of water would drown their noise.
So though we don't know what it means,
we listen as if to prayers to the
epitaph of the geese, shh, shh.

If a songbird is raised without
hearing the song of his species
he will develop incomprehensible
vocal sounds never heard in nature.
                    The New York Times

Abnormal Song

Tired of our own voices asking
always the same question, sing-song,
the same preen in small talk,
bright feathers of the dialect

of longing, we learn less from birds
than we might have wished.
Gone to listen in a scrubbed field
in simplifying winter how less cold

a white-crown sings the day,
we don't hear normal song.
He's heard another melody
in tanner shrubs, his fellows singing

lower notes here over the hill.
He's never heard his own voice, may be,
and never modifying his glib whistle,
he's lone, outlined, in the leafless

oak tree. Awry as a bud
in the silver air. What are we to do?
The singular voice in the wind
falling on dead ears. Oh,

we cannot look openly
into each other's eyes. Neither dominant,
we look at a neutral place a few inches by
our faces, rock on our feet, breathe slant.

The bird warbles and warbles.

Sovereign Bear

There is a bear before us
we saw caged, lumberous;
ears fly-sore, coat darkened by the loss
of year-long snows

and by a residue of steel
when he resisted the wall.
Rocking to and fro, turtle-
necked, immovable

as a bolted-down toy,
he seemed momentarily
domesticated, until with a scary
suddenness he turned his lord's eye

on us and stood up pawing
the air, as though he could dig
himself through air out of our king-
dom, stretched big

as we might come to know
in his gross land of snow
and blood-hunger. Soul-
less, sovereign and so

cunning; his mammal beauty
makes us shudder. After his prey
has tried to flee
and felt the stinging, instinctual joy

of his claw swing,
this grim genius of killing
eats, perfected, to kill again.
For us there is nothing

everyday as vigilant or cruel.
We stand near his childish hemisphere, all
changelings admiring the final
brutishness behind the thin wall.

What legendary ice or extinction
now? The bear pads to his alien
hut and lolls on the ground
like an old tom, and we return

to the city, degrees warmer
in its center's misting glare.
If we can see it, what star
will point us to the mad perimeter,

the rime, where the beast learns
to walk almost like a woman or man?

Redbirds

The redbirds gathered
in the pines railing the hill
behind the house, the snow grew

colder and empyreal,
and the moon moved into place
in the east. Then

the flock swayed
and was gone, the horizon
crowned by empty iodine.

There were animal tracks
knee-deep, dark troughs
of snow to follow,

and sounds of wind, night's feints
white and stinging
in the rack of winter boughs.

As long as I walked in the absence
of the redbirds, my eyes attuned
to such vague cages

of light as were, shadows took
the shapes of Yeti
or winter lion,

frightening beyond sense,
but all the time going away.
I tried to look past

the dense dark,
beyond the close,
beyond whatever closes

when redbirds plunge off the crest
of a hill, but saw only
the chilly reaches of snow.

Who shall say
when I reach the crest of the hill,
the shadows will not be deep

and gray as now
and the world
not have an exit

but a farther field
waning west,
the winds off that snow

cold as fence wire, and no harp?

Cold Frame

Stray ends of light in the window
glimmer into a wan mosaic of my face,
the translucent forehead pressed on the pane.
I see through the delicate siege
of this ghost, visitor and visitant,
knowing darkness will take it back again,
a plum-colored haze wreathing the bushes,
and, just beyond the hedgerow in the yard,
snowfall blowing like torn parchment.

Apple blossoms are falling,
making a sour lyric of the snow,
and though green wavers of light
rise from the dooryard like spring,
this slant of drifting grains of ice,
like little crystal minutes, obscures
in gray weather the frail shoots.
Here I am again in winter:
the snow piles up on the window sill.

Underneath the roof of the chicken house
the soil simmered—paramoecia and melted
snow—but in such mildness as of dreams
that remind me in the mornings of something
not unpleasant and not totally formed.
On a day like this one, the unexpected
weight of snow caved in the chicken house,
and the ground next August
was a cornucopia of green weeds.

In a concentrated drop of distance
a robin makes a bickering dance on snow,
but nothing happens. The false weather
is brilliant in the light it sheds:
the hot-house snow protects the seedlings,
their soft, vagrant tangle. The hair-spring
work of the deepest cells continues
as if an unseen clock hung in the air.
The light always comes back.

The Bride

*Gustav Klimt died in 1918 after a stroke, leaving his last
painting on its easel, its principal figure half nude.*

On a day snow flicks and swirls
and the Danube lies like a great silver fish
the wind and waves can no longer jostle,
Klimt lies paralyzed as if the bare space in
    the hospital room
has let its weight down on his chest.
Soon he begins to see in the white-slaked walls
a subtle, almost graffito flower fill
and a woman unlike anyone he has ever met—the thigh,
the naked foot, and the stirred-up mists
of her shoulders and face. He thinks of his painting
The Bride and how beneath the scrolls and orange
    flowers
with their sconces full of sap, the hairs of his brush
caressed the girl. He'd begun to fill in the anatomy
of her skirt, stippling the fallen petals and the pollen
upon the baroque cloth to wrap her nude legs and pubis.
Smiling, he thinks of his lover Emilie in summer,
her surprise when she raised the well bucket
and found a salamander bobbing there, and how a
    garden
is rhythmically absorbed into a figure of a woman
in the sun. He closes his eyes to imagine
the rouged faces and pale translucency of breast
and limb entangled in ornate silks near the girl
whose unfinished face makes the beholder more aware
they are parts of her dream which swirl in space,

in color, just below the surface of her thought.
Klimt tries to sit up. He looks at the winter bouquet
of flowers on his bedstand. Tomorrow he'll color
the apparatus and light of these blossoms
on the girl's skin with the brush's very tip, he thinks,
taking his time so not to wake her in her dreamt garden
until all the ovals, spirals, swirls and triangles
tipped on their heads are worthy of a bride's reverie.
Only then will he know which qualities of her eyes,
smoky green with morning and rain or heavily lidded
as though from pollen, to bring to life. The woman
in the purity of the white wall waits, or seems to,
like a bride. Klimt wants her to dress and to remain
as if in a ceremony of sunlight, but reminded of her
    nakedness,
the marriage bed's, as he by gaslight on stone
and by the snow is aware of the bitter ease of the grave
beneath a bed of flowers. The next time he closes
    his eyes
he feels the earth open for him—the dark ajar,
the soil spangled with gold, an inert, unmoving flame—
and then a huge body, a blackness, has hold of him.

Lines Written in Manassas
Bull Run

What is Art? Not

a battlefield
where the high cold star is now

as years

before in place? Not light
making the retina etch
hills and trees in memory,

a slumbering landscape,
nor the absent toppled, the generations

of worms,

the bullets lodged in a Confederate tree?
It is cold and clear, preserving
those invisible

who lie with their swords and bones
in the bottom of a dream.

It is their heaven.

In art they wait for those who come
more or less to mourn

and scanning history's noiseless lot
imagine cannons,
then see

the trees rise
and thin away like ranks.

There must be ecstasy: The soldiers
must get to the top of the hill.

And protocol: They crumple
and fall from the grapeshot

like leaves out of season. Over and over
in art.

Art is the habit of this place.
In it the wounded tree
is wise,

and the ground is wise.
In it only the dead sleep.

The Winter Without Snow

The man carried bucket after bucket of plaster dust
up the earthen ramp of the barn that caught fire
and emptied each as if he were dumping snow
onto the blackened beams.
In the trees there were little glass seeds,
souvenirs of winter without snow.

When the man turned back toward the house,
he wore a helmet of dusty mother-of-pearl,
and his eyelashes were silvery half-moons.
I watched him with all the coldness I had,
yet it would not snow.

Nothing could make it snow.
Not the burst water pipes, the leggings,
the sleds, or the white horses.
Not the smoky fountains, the clouds.
They were souvenirs of winter without snow,
as was my wish for a white field
like a fresh beginning.

Notes to the Cold

The skies crumble like marl, and winter
makes fossils of trees. The light
is vault-gray. By a window a boy
plays his trumpet, high A's and C's
like yellow flowers blown inside-out
in a fierce wind. He wipes the spittle off
his mouthpiece and watches knotted sparrows
in nets of snow settle on a white filigree.
Then, as if his great aloneless could be
lofted through the searing gray continuum,
he serenades the snow, the cold blossom
of his trumpet, forever cold, slipping petal
after invisible petal through the window
and the sill. By every trick of light
they are invisible, like the carved initials
of his name encased in snow, but he shows
no sign of stopping, any more than birds
quit ramming their feathery heads
against the snow. And when he does stop,
all is as it was, or seems, unless the boy
is changed. He might be thinking of his father's
words meant as a challenge but not unkindly:
You quit and someone will take over.
He might have hoped one more note
would have emptied the sky of its last snow.
He puts the trumpet in its matter-
of-fact case—there again are his initials—
and walks to the window bluish with snow.
His breath makes a page where, preoccupied,

he draws a bird, fixing the tilt
of its wings so it can fly. Behind it
the black trees struggle in the wind,
the snow falls; through it he sees what's left
of daylight blossom and fade,
and then the bird is gone.

IV

The Migration of Butterflies

The green forest lanes that end
in the Mexican mountains
are strewn with monarch butterflies
this March; where the lanes
end, evergreens are covered
in yellow layers. Alone,
can you see these monuments,
vast as Stonehenge, and not think
of June's ticker-tape parade
beating north, and those fallen
along the way like a trail
of colorful bits left there
by someone gone in the woods
too far and never come back?

In oblivion, the wind
with its light hands can scatter
several of the butterflies,
as a sleeping pensioner
can brush away the small flies
from this face, shift, and still sleep.
The chilled monarchs spiral down,
calm as spring showers of snow-
flakes. Too cold to wake them now!
The monuments, dear-achieved,
stand under a changing sky
where sunlight stirs in its time
all the resting butterflies.
For some the awakening
is early, for others late.

The Gardener Praises Rain

Beginning is the rain,
orphic, pausing at the orchard's brink
before the gardener gathers his tools
and hurries to the shed
and tanagers disappear into the purple breeze
near the peach trees,
then minor flutters in the leaves,
swaying boughs, a far break of waves,
and chutes
of sea-green and gray air. The tin
roof rails, and the gardener
shouts and drums
his hand rake on the wall, in rhythm
with the wild and turning earth
where all the peach buds, noiselessly,
are about to be released.

The Gardener Envies Henri Rousseau

The sun red gold, the people and animals
ripening in dark
green garden where the world is
made, what kind of bird untroubled
by the wind, sighing beyond the gardener's song:
The gardener dreams. Then wakes where round-eyed
lions no longer fit the shadows,
but a slow traveling
of light from roots to corn silk
reveals the worm and beetle.
So the dawn is ruled
by dew, by the all-day bird,
and by the gardener's rows of eggplant
shot purple. The gardener thinks only Rousseau
can paint the eyelids ever
green against the turning
of native leaves to snow.

Mallard

I raked up a mallard in the garden,
its body rolled in dirt.
It was as though I dragged
from its molded hill a large tuber
with eyes and buds for growth.
A horsefly landed on my leg
and a stink filled my nostrils.
Then the whole garden, dirt and air,
gave way to the death, as a birdflock,
thick at the center and jagged at the edges,
with a slight but irresistible movement,
veers south above a stubble field
or the sun enters the world.
The black feathers coruscated,
the garden was driven black,
and the breast went up
like the breaths of the just-born
or the sweet howling of the dog
that buried it.

Klimt's Baby

In a salt marsh
among a texture of weeds
a baby lies.
A woman has just left.
The sea changes color
all day. Nobody speaks
or comes. The baby listens
to its own cries. Eels
are hidden in the evening
shallows.
We know there is danger
in the black barge of
clouds that comes this way,
but we must wait, we think,
for the woman to come back.
We concentrate
on the pure, patient
face of the child.
And we tell ourselves
the sea is a quilt,
the quilt the baby wears
is a calm sea,
the baby will live.

The Gardener Delivers a Fawn

Raking the springbrook
clear of branches, water rolling its trasparent bells
down the moss and stones, the gardener
sees the light wheel on its hinge
and close, though some things sneak through.
He finds in shadows thin as broth
the pelvis of a deer. A doe,
he thinks, remembering the nippled belly
of one he hit with his car in the star-shattered
night last fall. He bent near and counted six nipples
before her eyes blinked wide
with no more fear. Then the belly wobbled.
He slit the furry sphere with his pocket knife
and found the fawn, which kept it firm
and sound like the stone inside a peach, only wetter,
and put his hand into the blood
to free the fawn, small
as a rabbit, with ears that large,
but with its spots. The fawn died
with its mother, eyelids translucent and closed.
He stood back from the fresh gusts of sweetness
cast up from the two deer. It was very dark,
and his red hand cooled.

Constellation

Again the lilacs
smell like new decay.
Here in the living room
and out on the bushes

the white and purple
stars spoil in clusters,
reminding of curdled
milk and blood's platelets

which some people drink,
plugging a cow's vein
and draining one udder
for nourishment. A death

is only beautiful
if we concentrate
on distances, neither
east nor south, but somewhere

through vegetation
of lights and small pools
where the fatted lilacs
echo the stars' ferment.

Passage

Held off and drawn by ordinary
differences, as if a lens were pushed
out of focus, or the diverging blue threads
on a map were the directions of impatience,
I tell myself,

here is a raven, yellow beak,
ringed eyes, sleek, in the graveyard
grown so tame for crumbs, its predecessor
lies under a country verse.

Let your giving-looks, like the sameness
of prize orchids, breed or wither
in their own season.
I remember snow in May—
breath after breath of petals
strewed the ground.
Our eyes could not unmake it.

The only fidelity
is in our fingertips tracing
and retracing the exact passage of the veins
of the throat. And love, once spoken,
comes with a wing held over the heart.

Aubade of an Early Homo Sapiens
like none other before

In this lonely, varying light
of dawn with the residue of desire
like mist departing, I am walking.
Was it in your eyes, where my elongated face shone,
I saw for the first time,
as if all the transparent fire in these trees
had become palpable,
a hunger that was not wholly animal?

The need to tremble like dogwood, feeling the rain
    touch down.
My strange blood rises, and I may
see you, fair leaves slipping over you, half-hidden
in the morning. With the beasts
beside a pond, I conjure the inward sun
to leap into my brain. What remains?
Wild, beautiful petals all around.
A beast's face. And something, something else.

Our Night

Deep in the night, the desk
and armchair dim guardians,
no sound but the peaceful breathing
of ourselves,

we begin slowly to make love,
touching each other everywhere water
bathes the rose.

When my cries are borne gently
on the dark air and fall,

I wonder, is this the last time?

Country Marriage

They married out of school
when she could feel the baby's feet
fixed deep inside and feel
her passion quicken for the sweet

romance. He bought on time
a trailer on an ugly hill
and worked in town sometimes.
She leaned her forehead on the sill

and watched him tune the car
and vowed she cared for living things.
She saw how everywhere
the pollen cast its nets and strong

buds splashed a little color
onto the waving greenery,
then didn't mind the squalor
of axles, oil pans, grease, and flies.

She loved the honeysuckle,
the running light across the land;
she made herself a necklet
and spoke to him in tones of lead.

A quick in time, a bead
of blood, and dumb imaginings
became their solitude.
Their yard filled up with junk and rings

of rainbow in the ditch
they got their drinking water from.
She didn't care so much.
She didn't care if he stayed home.

When summer turned to ash
a little witless sheep was born,
child slow to be itself
which lay in a crib all alone

caught up in their neglect.
She saw the bitter apple tree
and gutted car perfect
in winterfall, and senselessly

an equilibrium
held them something like love that year.
The child held in its arms
a sour doll. They had come far.

One More

Always you want more
than is your portion,
to take on your plate

before the others
more potatoes, more meat,
to plead if you must

for another chance,
another kiss, but
never to get quite

enough, whatever
you steal, work, promise
for. Always failing

to have your own way,
imagining times
two the dimensions

of your days and needs.
The mirror you look
into buries you

with the elements
you most want to keep
and can't. Small wonder

when love or hungers
start, like lights kindling
surfaces to brief

life, then snuffing out,
you take for yourself
with *now* and *once more*

what there is.

Two Poems / Toward Silence

I. As I slept

Moment by hopeless moment
you stared at my relaxed stranger's face.
Of the wind's rattle, and tumult of sea
mounting the esplanade,
that failed to rouse me,
you thought only it was time to go.
I woke before you crossed the muffled floor,
and saw the prison of your eyes,
gray and set, no gesture of love unlocks.
And as the storm leaked in the spaces,
scarcely aloud you said my name,
goodbye. Then. Nothing
but the click of the downstairs door.

II.　　Your letter

　　　　. . . our bodies
　　　　without intercession of word or thought,
　　　　you write.
　　　　　　　　　　　　Out the window
　　　　the trees are clotting light; their scripts
　　　　across the snow disclose no meaning,
　　　　yet pose the shifting of moments
　　　　toward June. And beneath the snow
　　　　no equivalents for flowers: Ox-Eye,
　　　　Bleeding Heart, Our-Lord's-Candle.
　　　　I cannot ever touch you and not want to ask
　　　　your name for this possession,
　　　　something like light caged in snow, and heat.
　　　　I cannot bear your answer
　　　　and cannot come there.

Exotic Dancer

Now there is a spotlight on the oaken bar.
Off comes her netting. She begins
to ravel, portions of her anatomy
shifting into different states.

Her body is, by parable, a man's rib
turned by longing into something more
sinewy and soft. Then made chaste
by a dress of fig leaf.

Barefoot, now, in the briefest panties
imaginable, she dances, the sequins
on her tits like the eyes of a fish,
and some of the bar's patrons turn away

out of respect, or the deep revulsion of flesh.
Say something that refuses to show
itself, that cannot be called a name
like *joy* or *snake*, informs

this exotic dance. Thinking the pronominal
possible, how can you not applaud,
even as she tucks her head between her legs
or hugs herself like a man?

What can we give each other or dance
lift from us, but the temporal:
limbs juxtaposed on a beer-stained stage
for once and for ever lovely.

Unfinished Song

All day long, before the sun sings a requiem,
I walk through the thicket-rich hills
along deer paths where the finely cleft hooves
make wells in the mud, and the peace of mind
of water under grasses is sung quietly.
The green smell of grass and water rises.
And a tympani of savannah sparrows
plays in the glazed trees.
All day long, all along a stream
mottled with shadows,
whose pulse is felt in the wood finger
dancing at the surface, through lyric hollows,
each different from the last, fish like pebbles
piling on each other.
All day long, intoxicated by odors and songs
of damp earth, the soft panting
of earth's withers,
I walk to forget
the simplest song,
lips scarcely parted,
the last note of lament unfinished:
Is there a solitude greater
than the solitude of shadows cast into water
like black tissue? Only the O
of the moon, not empty but in mind,
above my companion's shoulder
in a world of beginning
and blossoms
so soon gone.

book was set in Century Book on
a offset. One thousand copies were
ty)   and coordinated in Memphis, Ten-
nesse   by Gayle Cooke/TypeMasters and
prir   d by Jaco-Bryant Printing Company.
The poet signed and numbered twenty-five
c   es.